American Suite

A Literary History of the United States

poems by

Steven G. Kellman

Finishing Line Press
Georgetown, Kentucky

American Suite

A Literary History of the United States

ACKNOWLEDGMENTS

I am grateful to the editors of *Light,* in which "him" and "Buzzing Fly" first
appeared.

Publisher: Leah Maines

Editor: Christen Kincaid

Cover Art: John S. Dykes

Author Photo: Calvin Hoovestol

Cover Design: Elizabeth Maines McCleavy

Printed in the USA on acid-free paper.
Order online: www.finishinglinepress.com
            also available on amazon.com

Author inquiries and mail orders:
Finishing Line Press
P. O. Box 1626
Georgetown, Kentucky 40324
U. S. A.

Table of Contents

"It takes a great deal of history to produce a little literature."

Henry James

Poor Benjamin

Thank Ben Franklin,
Patriotic sage, for
The bifocal, the lightning rod,
And the local library.
But the story wasn't always merry.
Though his work as Founding Father
Earned Ben enduring glory,
His own son William
Chose to be a Tory.

Free to Starve

Phillis Wheatley wrote so sweetly
Boston elders affirmed her rhymes.
Free men praised her luscious lines.
Emancipated by her master's will,
She found that poems won't pay the bills.

Common Sense

The bane of royalists, loyalists, and
Swells intent on private gain,
Thomas Paine deserved his name.
The common sense that he dispensed
Spurred colonists to independence—
Though stern John Adams of Braintree, Mass.
Called his work "a crapulous mass."
Paine disdained the privileged classes,
Particularly priests. He proclaimed
That man could not be free
While shackled to a deity.
Even in the Age of Reason,
Attacking God was vilest treason.
Pious cads denied a grave to Paine's remains.

Father of the American Novel Fond of Filicide

Charles Brockden Brown gained renown
By bringing gothic horror to America.
Brown's homicidal maniacs cannot be trusted,
Though Wieland's father was done in
Not by a beastly son but spontaneous combustion.
Brown conjured up a world of heinous, haunted rivals.
His style is fustian,
His subject graveyards and their busy shovels.
He pioneered the native novel.

Sleeping Through the Revolution

Slumbering subject of a distant king,
Rip Van Winkle fell
Into sleep so deep
He could not hear the village bells.
Four decades later,
He awakened to a novel fate:
Senior citizen of the United States.

The Pioneers

It isn't batty or even catty
To jump from Natty Bumppo and Chingachgook
To famous books with mixed-race mates.
Trace the ways that Queequeg, Jim, and Tonto
Bond with their fawning, fond white-skinned chums.
For some, like Leslie Fiedler, not mere amity
But something queer sums up the nation's aspirations.
Nevertheless, appalled by counting bloopers,
Mark Twain was drugged into a stupor
Struggling through the prose of Fenimore Cooper.

Mired in Muck at Brook Farm

Because his forebear made the witches hang,
Life for Hawthorne held no tang.
On every stranger's cheek he saw a scar
To remind him of how vile we are.

American Scholar

A pastor on a soulful search,
Emerson deserted Boston's Second Church.
Rejecting Communion was not defiance,
Instead the start of self-reliance.

Transcendentalist Utopia

We have to do without a lot,
Warned Fruitlands leader Bronson Alcott.
No meat, no money, no milk, no honey.
Fruitlands' name was clearly moot.
With only ten bare apple trees,
Utopia hardly bore much fruit.

Henry David Thoreau

Walden Pond is now a beach
Beyond the reach of solitude.
While Thoreau lived,
A man could still make good
By living life fully in the woods.
When that seemed stale,
He spent a night in Concord jail.

Life at Sea

Shipped out on a brig with ordinary gobs,
Richard Henry Dana—no snob—
Forsook his privileged caste.
The pay was mean, the food was nasty,
The work befit a dog.
When two mates made demands,
They were flogged.
Four years passed on land,
And, Dana's memory jogged,
He answered with *Two Years Before the Mast.*

Of Books and Wars

Uncle Tom was not an Uncle Tom.
He came to harm
By refusing to lash a fellow slave.
Stowe's brash book made readers rave.
Uncle Tom was a bomb
Tossed at a world that none could save.

Misinformed

Herman Melville
At the Wailing Wall.

Rags to Riches

With pluck and luck,
His spunky Yankee soared above the flock.
The self-made man, a target of nostalgia:
The author, not his hero, was named Horatio Alger.

Buzzing Fly

I heard a fly buzz when I died—
It broke the peace and hurt my pride.
The hateful seamstress—Refuse to tip her!
Left me—with a noisy zipper.

I Never Saw a Moor

I never saw a Moor
Until I saw *Othello.*

End of Debate on the Great American Novel

A boy on a raft on a river.
Did ever an author write as well?
You say yes?
All right, then, you go to hell.

Sarah Orne Jewett

Mainer mavens always knew it.
The local bard was Sarah Jewett.
Concede the credit where it is hers.
She wrote *The Country of the Pointed Firs.*

The Lesson of the Master

Young Henry James was racked
With shame. He used his back
To shun the flaming battle front.
He later blamed America for
Staying out of Europe's war.
In a culminating snit,
Henry James became a Brit.

Stephen Crane

Stephen Crane stalked Bowery streets
Taking notes on streetwalkers.
He sailed to the tropics to track other topics.
Three days in an open boat,
And he felt he would croak.
Safer to write of courage
In a gory war
That ended six years before
Stephen Crane was even born.

An Education in Henry Adams

If I were Henry Adams,
I would not be I.
Why? Adams was a lot like you and me,
Except preferred the pronoun he.

The Jungle Bungled

Upton Sinclair relished raking muck
To show wage slaves how they are stuck.
He sought defeat for corporate leaders,
But readers merely gave up meat.

Where is Ethan From?

To the manner born, Edith Wharton
Scorned the trappings—and the traps—
Of her elevated native social class.
The patroons of Wharton's narrow world
Deemed it crass and crude
To live above 14th Street
Or eat Italian food.
Wharton mocked those girls
Whose only goal is snatching spouses.
Yet her own first book
Was called *The Decoration of Houses.*

O, Pioneer!

If you had asked her,
Willa Cather, living in Manhattan,
Would have admitted that
She never truly left Nebraska.
The task she could not refuse
Was neither trite nor sundry.
Like Virgil, she was the first
To invite the Muse into her country.

Brother Theodore

When Clyde tried to break
With poor dear Roberta
(I swear he never meant to hurt her!),
She sank beneath a clear Adirondack lake,
And Clyde expired in the electric chair.
Wealth and class to him were magic.
For Dreiser, only somewhat wiser,
It was all American, and tragic.

Poet Overboard

Hart Crane should have gone by train.
His Aztec epic reduced to nought,
He turned to booze and boys and
A homeward vessel docked at port.
Precious poets, do not despair
Over hindrances to making art.
Or, like the steamship *Orizaba*,
You might lose Hart.

Hilda Doolittle

Born in Bethlehem (PA),
She made her name H.D.
The empress of Imagism
Whose noiseless line
Neither clots nor cloys,
Hilda Doolittle did a lot.
She loved both girls and boys.

Stein is Stein is Stein is Stein

Survival on the line,
Gertrude Stein played her chances
And stayed in Vichy France.
"I am fussy about food,"
She explained.
Return to Oakland would be too crude.
There's no *beurre* there.

The Great Gatsby

Jimmy Gatz sat on the dock of the bay
Pining for the green light
That shone through the gray.
Was he deranged?
Did he not know
The light had changed?

The Sage of Baltimore

A connoisseur of kvetch,
H.L. Mencken made jolly mockery
Of the wretched follies of the booboisie.
He aimed his darts
At the complacent state of Moronia,
Though he was part.
Most today would share his views,
Except on gays and Jews.

The Vicious Circle

The fabled Algonquin wits
Traded quips over sober soup
Set atop their own round polished table.
If you were able,
Would you not love to sit for lunch
With that jaded, faded, boozy bunch?
Did they discard their inhibitions?
Hardly. Remember Prohibition.

Babbitt, Run

Crowned in Stockholm, Sinclair Lewis said:
Others should have made the trip instead.
He smote the smug and fought the fight.
About his standing he was right.

Spanish Poet in New York

García Lorca was no New Yorker.
Even months at Columbia—¡Ay, caramba!—
Couldn't teach him much of English.
In vermilion Castilian he described
The city's rhythm, its geometry, its anguish.
He observed the Wall Street crash
And the Harlem Remuerte.
Except for his unquenchable duende,
He might have languished in Madrid
And never crossed the Brooklyn Bridge,
Nor written *Poeta en Nueva York*.
Back at home in Spain,
García Lorca was a rising star
Shot to death by fascists outside Alfacar.

Pound Foolish

Lordly impresario of the vagrant avant-garde,
Ezra Pound found it hard to stanch his rage
Against the stench of usury and Jews.
He wrote *The Pisan Cantos* in a cage.

The *Life* Luce Saved

Henry Luce distilled the weekly news
Into a tidy packet he called *Time*.
To please Clare Booth, his wife,
Luce spent more than ninety grand
To resuscitate a thing called *Life*.
Readers in a lower bracket
Could buy it for a dime.

Countee Cullen

A Renaissance man,
Harlem brand,
Countee Cullen tried his hand
At Latin, Greek, and drama.
His mama disappeared for twenty years.
He put in words the fears too often shaped by race.
Countee Cullen is not an Irish place.

him

within the circles cummings traveled
pious thoughts came all unraveled
while others raved at capitalist tools
he saved his rage for majuscules

Complacencies of the Penal System

Monday morning,
Wallace Stevens goes to court.
He did something no one ought.
How, when law defines litter,
Can beauty hold a plea?
He placed a jar in Tennessee.

The Roads All Taken

Two roads diverged in a wood, and I
Took both, which is why
There are no roads left in the yellow wood,
Which, for the health of sylvan growth,
Is for the good, is for the good.

On to California

Tom Joad shoulda knowd.
No point in movin' farther west
Where nothin' feeds
But Rose of Sharon's swollen breast.
When all your native dreams have turned to dust,
There ain't no farm boss you can trust.

Papa H.'s Waltz

That author's fondest, fatal wish:
Prose reduced to verbs and nouns,
Life reduced to drink, punch, hunt, and fish.
Economy of expression,
Etiology of terminal depression.

Which Way Does the Wind Blow?

Margaret Mitchell dreamed of Tara,
A misty vanished world where
A selfish harlot named O'Hara
Gets pampered by Mammy, Pork, and Prissy.
Why are the differences so stark?
They are black, and she is Scarlett.

Mississippi Misanthropes

Ab and Flem and Byron Snopes
Live to cheat more honest folks.
Clarence and his kin know far too well
How to coax a man to hang himself,
If they supply the ropes.

Marianne Moore

Marianne Moore adored
Pangolins, hornbills, porcupines—
Hornèd creatures hard to handle.
She also worshipped Mickey Mantle.
Asked by Ford to name a car,
She was not meek.
She offered: Mongoose Civique.
Rejecting with thanks a sure hard sell,
They went instead for Edsel.

Native Son

Bigger Thomas burned a body in a furnace.
It was a crime.
It wasn't right.
Doing harm was never Bigger's true intent.
How was he to know just what he meant?
The author, Richard Wright,
Refused to turn his cheek
When rednecks tweaked it,
Or turn his back on fellow blacks.
G-men stalked the author even into France.
Of what did Richard die?
Maybe heart disease, or cancer.
No chance, said daughter Julia.
It was the FBI.

Word Slinger Isaac Singer

I.B. Singer foresaw the danger.
Rather than linger in Warsaw,
He left behind, in a blink,
Wife and son—the stinker!—
And came to reside on the Upper West Side.
He wrote about demons and dybbuks,
Hungry maidens and skittish scholars.
Did he ever write a clinker?
Did Stalin daven mincha?
Was his fiction British?
Zikher nisht. He wrote in Yiddish.

Out of Step with Pencey Prep

He says that swell old Sally Hayes
Is a royal pain in the ass.
He knows he's not insane.
But, held in the booby hatch,
Holden starts to lose his sass.
Who'll be there to catch
A body coming through the rye?
What really kills him
Is that everyone's phony,
Save for Phoebe and the ducks in Central Park.
Yet it's dark and lonely
To try to live without a lie.

Norman Mailer: Success and Failure

Wrenched from the steps of the Pentagon,
Norman Mailer sassed his jailer.
He knifed his wife and ran for mayor.
He boozed and brawled.
His list of flaws was rather long.
He also wrote *The Executioner's Song.*

The Misfits

Summoned by HUAC to name names,
Arthur Miller never cowered, never snitched.
He mustered his dramatic knack to write a play
That shamed the Salem powers who placed
A noose around the necks of those defamed
By being branded Satan's witch.

Hammett's Ghost

This is hard-boiled hell.
Cons on the make,
Cops on the take,
Vice and sleaze to sell.
Raw survival is at stake.
Dashiell Hammett's Continental Op
Tries to tell the true from fake.
Hammett calls Sam Spade Sam Spade.
Paid to smell the human stench,
He left his scent on the writer's trade.

Louisiana Williams

Pity pretty Blanche DuBois.
The snooty wench has lost her mind.
She also lost Belle Reve, the family manse.
Never depend on strangers to be kind.

Mr. Bellow's Planetarium

Artur Sammler outlived Himmler.
One eye shuttered by a rifle butt,
Mr. Sammler clutches shards of memory
And broods about the new barbarity.
He calls himself a registrar of madness.
Sorry for all and sore at heart,
He's almost glad to end the story.

A Supermarket in California

Walt Whitman in the produce aisle
Smiles at Allen Ginsberg pawing tangerines.
Poets who howl need piles to eat.
Kerouac, Corso, Burroughs, and Snyder
Crave something that's sweeter than tart apple cider.
To savor the borscht you need to squeeze Beets.

Baldwin Grand

James Baldwin came to fame
When race replaced place
As a writer's ID.
He grew up in Harlem,
And settled in France.
But a superficial glance
Saw only an angry colored man.
Declining to give up the fight,
Baldwin chided:
"I'm only black
Because you think you're white."

Wise Blood

Flannery O'Connor at her desk
Calmly conjured up grotesque
Specimens of the human race
Who, locked in confusion,
Mock the actions of God's grace.
A flock of peacocks at Andalusia Farm—
Calm intimations of the Parousia.
This O'Connor knew:
Human horror masquerades as honor.

Confessional

Anyone can do the math:
Ted's deific bees, the helpless kids,
The winter trees.
And last the gas.
Subtract the bliss from Sylvia Plath.

The Day Frank O'Hara Died

It is 6:00 a.m. on Fire Island, a Sunday
Nine days after Bastille Day, yes
It is 1966, and Mao swims the Yangtse,
But the beach breathes peace.
Easy to laugh at what would become an epitaph:
"Grace to be born and live
As variously as possible,"
Wrote Frank O'Hara,
Soon crushed beneath a dune buggy,
While we all were out to sea
And poetry and he stopped breathing

Kesey's Great Notion

Too tough to handle or set free on bail,
Randle McMurphy swaggers out of jail
And into something worse,
A psychiatric ward whose lord
Is the tyrant called Big Nurse.
The wretched refuse of fascist Ratched,
They fear the thought of open clashes
Until McMurphy leads an insurrection.
Though one man, Bromden, flies the coop,
The struggle brings grim trouble to the group.
Upon reflection, it might have worked out best
For most to stay within their nest.

Yonnondio

Why did Tillie Olsen publish little?
In asking that,
I tell no riddles.
Born a Lerner,
She caught on quickly
That ironing family linen
And winning prickly union fights
Left scant time to breathe or write.

Prolific Harper Lee

To Kill a Mockingbird—its author's first.
It was her best.
It was her worst.
Harper Lee wrote perfectly.
No need, she reckoned,
To write a second.

Styron's Choice

Depression, quipped William Styron,
Is a wimp of a word
For a howling tempest in the brain.
Blamed for channeling a Nazi victim
And a rebel slave,
He growled that art is indivisible.
Styron made the darkness visible.

Philip Roth's Complaint

It wasn't true.
Yet in shuls and schools,
Over tablecloths stained
By thick spare ribs and shrimp chow mein,
More than a few mavens
Proclaimed Philip Roth:
A self-hating Jew.
Like moths to menorahs,
Roth was lured to mock
Mah jongg, lox, and mink,
Though he'd really rather think
About the link between sex and
Personal extinction. He loved biting
The hand that fed folks chazzerei.
Almost out of spite,
The JTS granted Roth an honorary distinction,
After he had ceased to write.

Steven G. Kellman served four terms on the board of directors of the National Book Critics Circle and is a recipient of the NBCC's Nona Balakian Citation for Excellence in Reviewing. *American Suite* is his first collection of poetry, but his other books include *Redemption: The Life of Henry Roth* (Norton); *The Translingual Imagination* (Nebraska); *Loving Reading: Erotics of the Text* (Archon); and *The Self-Begetting Novel* (Columbia). A contributing writer to *The Texas Observer*, he has published in a variety of other venues, including *American Scholar, Atlantic Monthly, Bookforum, Chronicle of Higher Education, Georgia Review, Gettysburg Review, Michigan Quarterly Review, The Nation, New England Review, The New York Times Book Review, Southwest Review,* and *Virginia Quarterly Review*. Kellman has taught at the University of California campuses of Berkeley and Irvine, Tel-Aviv University, Tbilisi State University, and the University of Sofia and is a professor of comparative literature at the University of Texas at San Antonio. He is married to the poet Wendy Barker.

www.ingramcontent.com/pod-product-compliance
Lightning Source LLC
Chambersburg PA
CBHW021201090426
42740CB00008B/1182